The Save Our Spire

L.O.A.F. Recipe Book

A Selection Of Tasty
Local, Organic, Animal-friendly Or
Fairtrade Recipes
From
St Ives Free Church And Friends.

INTRODUCTION

Thank you on behalf of the SOS team for purchasing this recipe book to raise money for repair of the spire of the Free Church (United Reformed) St Ives.

We are a Fairtrade and Eco-church and care of the environment is very important to us.

To this end, our recipe book follows these L.O.A.F. principles whenever possible.

L = Locally-produced.
O = Organic.
A = Animal friendly.
F = Fairly-traded.

We encourage you to do the same by shopping locally and using locally grown ingredients.

All our recipes are kindly donated by members of the Free Church and their friends to whom we extend our grateful thanks.

We would like to send a special thank you to all who attended the garden party in July, from where we gathered many of these recipes. The winning entry in the cake competition, '3-layer Blueberry and White Chocolate Cake with Lemon and Lime', features on our front cover. Recipes accompanied by photographs are of cakes from the garden party.

CONTENTS   **PAGE**

CONVERSION CHARTS

Recipes in this book are presented as they were supplied, i.e. using both metric and imperial weights and measures. The following tables are supplied to offer conversions if they are needed.

Oven temperatures

Gas Mark	F	C
1	275	140
2	300	150
3	325	170
4	350	180
5	375	190
6	400	200
7	425	220
8	450	230
9	475	240

Weights

Ounce oz	Grams g
½	10
1	25
2	50
3	75
4	110
6	175
8	225
10	275
12	350
1 lb	450
1½lb	700
2	900

Volume

Fluid oz	Millilitre ml
2	55
3	75
5 – ¼ pint	150
10 – ½ pint	275
15 – ¾ pin t	425
20 – 1 pint	570

VICTORIA SPONGE

225g Fairtrade caster sugar.
225g sunflower margarine.
200g self-raising flour.
25g cornflour.
4 large free-range eggs.
2 tablespoons raspberry jam.
Fresh raspberries for decoration.

Method:
Mix caster sugar and margarine together to make a smooth mixture.
Add eggs and stir.
Sieve flour and cornflour together and add slowly to the mixture and fold in with a metal spoon to get a mixture which just about stays on the spoon.

Share the mixture into two 8-inch sponge tins and place in the middle of a pre-heated oven for approximately 20 – 25 minutes or until golden brown.
Gas mark 4 or 180 degrees C.

Wait until cool before removing from tins. Put on a wire rack until cold.

Spread the jam on one sponge and place the other sponge on top. Finish off with a sprinkling of caster sugar and decorate with fresh raspberries.

VICTORIA SPONGE

WELSH CAKES

225g self-raising flour.
1 pinch of salt.
110g sunflower margarine.
50g Fairtrade caster sugar.
50g Fairtrade currants or mixed fruit.
2 tablespoons of milk.
1 medium free-range egg.

Method:
Mix flour and salt together.
Rub in margarine until the mixture resembles breadcrumbs.
Stir in the sugar and fruit.
Mix to a fairly stiff dough with the egg and milk.
Roll out to about 5mm in thickness and cut into rounds.

Bake on a moderately hot, greased griddle or heavy frying pan for 2-3 minutes each side or until golden brown.

Dust with sugar if you wish.

ROCK BUNS

225g self-raising flour.
150g sunflower margarine.
150g Fairtrade caster sugar.
175g Fairtrade currants.
1 free-range egg.
A little milk.

Method:
Rub margarine and flour together until like breadcrumbs.
Add sugar, beaten egg and milk to make a stiff consistency.
Stir in currants.

Grease and flour baking tray.
Put heaps of the mixture onto the baking tray about 2cm apart.
Dust lightly with caster sugar.

Bake in oven, Gas mark 7 or 220 degrees C for 10 minutes.

Remove from tray and allow to cool on a wire rack.

LEMON, LIME & GINGER CHEESECAKE

Base:
200g ginger nut biscuits.
60g unsalted butter, melted.
Grated zest of 1 lime.
Vegetable oil.

Filling:
560g full fat cream cheese.
397g tin of condensed milk.
3 tablespoons stem ginger syrup.
Zest & juice of 2 lemons.
Zest & juice of 2 limes, save some zest for decoration.
1 sachet of gelatin (or vegetarian substitute).

Method:
Base: Crush the biscuits into fine crumbs, add the melted butter and lime zest and mix thoroughly.
Press all but 2 tablespoons of the crumbs into a lightly oiled 20 cm loose-bottomed cake tin.
Put in fridge to chill while making the filling.

Filling: Put all the filling ingredients, except the gelatin, into a large mixing bowl and mix until very smooth.
Prepare gelatin according to the instructions on the packet and then stir into the filling mixture.
Pour the filling on top of the biscuit base and cover with cling film.
Chill in fridge for at least 5 hours.
Remove cheesecake from tin and sprinkle with the spare biscuit crumb and lime zest.

LEMON, LIME & GINGER CHEESECAKE

BAKEWELL TART

Ingredients:
Shortcrust pastry:
225g plain flour.
1 pinch salt.
110g sunflower spread.
2 tablespoons cold water.
Raspberry jam.

Filling:
50g sunflower spread.
50g Fairtrade caster sugar.
1 large free range egg, beaten.
Few drops of almond extract.
10g ground almonds.
40g Fairtrade self-raising flour.
Flaked almonds for decoration.
Icing sugar, to dust.

Method:
Pastry: Add salt to flour and mix.
Rub sunflower spread into plain flour to make "breadcrumbs".
Add enough water to form a stiff dough.
Knead lightly for a few minutes, wrap in cling film and
refrigerate for 15 minutes.

Filling: Cream sunflower spread and sugar together until light and fluffy.
Blend in the egg and almond extract and then fold in the ground almonds
And self-raising flour.

Roll out pastry to slightly less than a centimetre (¼ inch) thick.
Line the pastry into a non-stick loose- based flan tin.
Trim excess pastry.

Spread the jam evenly over the pastry base.

Carefully spoon the filling mixture over the jam and spread
Into an even layer. Sprinkle over with flaked almonds.

Bake for 25-30 minutes until well risen and golden brown.
Gas mark 5 or 190 degrees C.

Leave to cool on a rack and dust with icing sugar.

COCONUT CAKES

75g sunflower margarine.
75g Fairtrade caster sugar.
50g self-raising flour.
50g Fairtrade desiccated coconut.
1 free-range egg.
A little milk.

Method:
Cream the margarine and sugar together until smooth.
Stir in the egg, flour, coconut and enough milk so that it is not too runny.
Spoon into individual baking cases.

Bake at gas mark 6, 200 degrees C, for 10-12 minutes.

CHOCOLATE MALTESER CAKE

Ingredients:
For the cake:

150g Fairtrade soft light brown sugar.
100g Fairtrade caster sugar.
3 free-range eggs.
175 ml milk.
15g butter.
2 tablespoons Horlicks.
175g Fairtrade plain flour.
25g Fairtrade cocoa, sieved.
1 teaspoon baking powder.
½ teaspoon bicarbonate of soda.

For the icing:

250g Fairtrade icing sugar
1 teaspoon Fairtrade cocoa
45g Horlicks.
125g soft unsalted butter.
2 tablespoons boiling water.
2 x 37g packets Maltesers.

Method: Cake:

Whisk together the sugars and the eggs.

Heat the milk, butter and Horlicks in a saucepan until the butter melts (do not let it boil).

Beat the hot Horlicks mixture in with the sugars and eggs.

Fold in the flour, cocoa, baking powder and bicarbonate of soda.

Line two 20cm loose-bottomed sandwich cake tins with greaseproof paper.

Divide the cake mix between the two tins and bake in the oven for 25 minutes.

Gas mark 3 or 170 degrees C.

Cool on a rack for 10 minutes and turn out of their tins.

Method: Icing:

Stir the icing sugar, cocoa and Horlicks together.

Add butter and carefully beat in.

Slowly add the boiling water and beat until you have a smooth buttercream.

Spread half the buttercream on each sponge. Put one on top of the other.

Make the top swirly rather than a smooth surface.

Decorate the top with Maltesers.

CHOCOLATE MALTESER CAKE

DUNDEE CAKE

The day before you make this cake, soak the fruit in a good sherry

175g sunflower margarine or butter.
175g Fairtrade light brown sugar.
4 free-range eggs.
225g wholemeal self-raising flour.
1 pinch of salt.
350g Fairtrade mixed dried fruit.
50g glace cherries.
Grated rind of 1 large orange.
3 tablespoons of flaked almonds.

Method:
Grease a deep 8" (20cm) tin and sprinkle with flour.
Cream the butter and sugar together.
Stir in eggs one at a time.
Add flour and mix together.
Fold in fruit and orange rind.
Spoon into cake tin and sprinkle almonds on top.

Bake for one hour, gas mark 4, 180 degrees C.
Then reduce the temperature to warm and continue to bake for another hour.

Remove from oven and leave to cool in the tin before turning out.

DUNDEE CAKE

EASY CHOCOLATE COURGETTE CAKE

250g plain flour.
375g Fairtrade caster sugar.
65g Fairtrade cocoa powder.
2 teaspoons bicarbonate of soda.
1 teaspoon baking powder.
1 teaspoon ground cinnamon.
4 free-range eggs.
350ml vegetable oil (ideally olive oil).
340g home or locally grown organic courgettes – grated.
100g chopped walnuts.

Method:
Stir everything together – it's as easy as that.
Cook in a 20 x 30 cm traybake tin suitably greased and lined.
Cook at approximately fan assisted 170 degrees C for about
an hour – checking to see if ready when a knife comes
out cleanly.
Add icing if desired.

ULTIMATE CHOCOLATE BROWNIES

370g Fairtrade caster sugar.
80g Fairtrade cocoa powder.
60g plain flour.
1 teaspoon baking powder.
4 free-range eggs, beaten.
250g unsalted butter, melted.
2 teaspoons vanilla extract.
100g Fairtrade dark chocolate.
100g Fairtrade white chocolate.

Method:
Stir the sugar, cocoa powder, flour and baking powder together in a large bowl.
Add the eggs, melted butter and vanilla extract and mix thoroughly.
Chop up chocolate into rough chunks and add to the mix.
Pour into a lined traybake tin and bake for 40-45 minutes.
Gas mark 2 ½ or 160 degrees C.
Leave to cool on a wire rack, then cut into squares.
Should make 16 Brownies.

LEMON CAKE

275g Fairtrade caster sugar.
3 free-range eggs.
120g olive oil.
275g self raising flour.
Juice of 3 lemons.

Method:
Whisk the sugar and eggs together.
Beat in the olive oil.
Beat in the lemon juice.
Fold in the flour.
(Add a little milk if mixture too stiff).

Spoon into a greased cake tin and bake for approximately
45 minutes,
Gas mark 4 or 180 degrees C.

LEMON CAKE

CHOCOLATE & BEETROOT CAKE

Ingredients:

For the cake:
250g cooked, peeled beetroot.
125g butter.
3 large free-range eggs.
1 pinch of salt.
A little water to slacken.
75g Fairtrade plain chocolate.
300g Fairtrade light brown sugar.
225g self-raising flour.
50g Fairtrade cocoa.

For the icing:
150g Fairtrade plain chocolate.
5 tablepoons Fairtrade icing sugar.
Grated white chocolate for decoration.
142ml sour cream.
3 tablespoons of Cassis.

Method: Cake:

Melt the chocolate over hot water.
Grate the beetroot coarsely.
Beat the butter, eggs and sugar until light and pale.
Add melted chocolate and fold in the flour, cocoa and beetroot.
Add a little water to slacken if necessary.
Pour into a greased 20 cm (8") tin and bake for approximately 45 -50 minutes.
Oven temperature gas mark 4 or 180 degrees C.
Leave to cool.

Method: Icing:

Put the chocolate, sour cream and icing sugar in a bowl over hot water.
Allow to melt, then beat well together.
Add Cassis.
Leave to cool, then ice the cake.
Cover with shavings of white chocolate.

COFFEE & WALNUT MUFFINS

For the cake:
175g soft butter or sunflower margarine.
175g Fairtrade caster sugar.
3 large free-range eggs.
65g chopped walnut pieces.
175g self-raising flour.
1 teaspoon baking powder.
2 teaspoons Fairtrade instant coffee granules.

For the topping:
75g soft butter or sunflower margarine.
150g icing sugar.
1 teaspoon Fairtrade instant coffee.
50g chopped walnut pieces.

Method: Cake:
Beat the butter and sugar together till light and fluffy.
Add the eggs a little at a time, beating well after each addition.
Sift the flour and baking powder together and fold into the mixture with a metal spoon.
Dissolve the coffee granules in a tablespoon of boiling water and stir into the cake mix.
Add the chopped walnuts and stir gently into the cake mixture.
Divide the mixture into 12 muffin cases.
Bake for 20-25 minutes, gas mark 4 or 180 degrees C.
Leave to cool in the cases. Transfer to a wire rack.

Method: Topping:
Beat the butter until pale and soft.
Add the sugar and beat until smooth and creamy.
Dissolve the coffee granules in 2 teaspoons of boiling water.
Mix into the buttercream.
When cool, spread each muffin generously with buttercream.
Sprinkle with chopped walnuts.

MINCEMEAT SLICES

110g sunflower margarine.
225g self-raising flour.
110g Fairtrade caster sugar.
1 beaten free-range egg.
3-4 tablespoons milk, to mix.
Jar of mincemeat.
Fairtrade brown sugar to finish.

Method:
Rub margarine into flour and stir in the sugar.
Make a well in the centre and pour in the egg and 3 tablespoons of milk.
Mix together gradually, adding more milk if necessary to give a soft dough.
Turn the mixture onto a floured board.
Divide into 2 and roll out each piece to 20cm square.
Lift one onto a greased baking sheet.
Spread with mincemeat (amount according to taste).
Leave a small border at the edges.
Place the other piece on top and press down firmly.
Brush with milk and sprinkle with brown sugar.
Bake at gas mark 5, 190 degrees C, for 20 minutes.

GUINNESS CAKE

225g butter.
225g Fairtrade soft brown sugar.
4 medium free-range eggs, lightly beaten.
275g plain flour.
2 level teaspoons mixed spice, sieved.
225g Fairtrade raisins.
225g Fairtrade sultanas.
110g mixed peel.
110g chopped walnuts.
8-12 tablespoons of Guinness.

Method:
Cream the butter and sugar together until light and creamy.
Gradually beat in the eggs.
Fold in the flour and spices.
Add raisins, sultanas, peel and walnuts.
Stir in 4 tablespoons Guinness and mix to a soft dropping consistency.

Turn into a prepared 7" cake tin.
Bake in oven gas mark 3, 170 degrees C, for one hour.
Reduce heat to gas mark 2, 150 degrees C and bake for a further 1 ½ hours.

Allow to cool and then remove from tin.
Prick base with skewer and spoon over the remaining Guinness.
Keep for a week before eating.

GUINNESS CAKE

INDIVIDUAL CARROT CAKES

For the cake:
250g Fairtrade light brown muscovado sugar.
200ml vegetable oil.
3 free-range eggs, beaten.
300g self-raising flour.
1 teaspoon cinnamon.
½ teaspoon ground ginger.
500g carrots, finely grated.
Zest of one orange, finely grated.
200g walnut pieces, roughly chopped.
200g Fairtrade sultanas.

For the icing:
175g icing sugar.
200g tub half-fat cream cheese.
1 – 1 ½ tablespoons orange juice.

Method: Cake:
Beat together sugar and vegetable oil for 2-3 minutes.
Add the eggs and mix well.
Sift in the flour and spices and mix well.
Stir in carrot, orange zest, walnuts and sultanas.

Spoon evenly into several baking cases.
Bake in oven, gas mark 4, 180 degrees C, for
25-30 minutes. Allow to cool.

INDIVIDUAL CARROT CAKES

Method: Icing
Sift icing sugar into a bowl.
Add the cream cheese and beat until combined.
Gradually add enough orange juice to form a spreadable consistency.
Spread evenly over the tops of each carrot cake.

GRANDMOTHER'S FRUIT CAKE

Written as grandmother used it, in imperial measure!

18oz mixed dried fruit.
6oz butter.
6oz brown sugar.
1 ½ teaspoons mixed spice.
12oz self-raising flour, sifted.
¼ pint water plus 3 tablespoons brandy.
3 large eggs, beaten.

Method:
Place the fruit, butter, sugar, water and brandy in a saucepan.
Simmer very gently for 20 minutes, then leave to cool.
Beat in the flour, mixed spice and eggs and mix well.
Pour into an 8" lined cake tin.
Bake at gas mark 2, 150 degrees C, for 1 ½ hours.

Leave to cool then remove from tin.

Decoration: This can be decorated as you wish. The cake shown was specially decorated for the Save Our Spire appeal.

GRANDMOTHER'S FRUIT CAKE

SUGARLESS FRUIT CAKE

225g Fairtrade sultanas.
300ml non-sweetened orange juice.
75g low-fat sunflower spread.
225g wholemeal self-raising flour.
1 teaspoon mixed spice.
2 free-range eggs, beaten.

Method:
Soak sultanas overnight in orange juice.
Mix the flour and spice together.
Rub the margarine into the flour until mixture resembles breadcrumbs.
Stir in the eggs, fruit and orange juice.
Turn the mixture into a 15cm greased and lined cake tin.
Bake at gas mark 4, 180 degrees C, for 1 ½ hours, or until a skewer pushed into the cake comes out clean.

BANANA BREAD

150g self raising flour.
¼ teaspoon bicarbonate of soda.
1 ripe Fairtrade banana.
50g soft butter.
1 free range egg.
150g Fairtrade caster sugar.
½ teaspoon vanilla essence.
pinch of salt.

Method:
Place egg, banana, sugar, butter, vanilla essence and salt in a liquidiser and blend on speed 3 to a smooth consistency.
Sieve the flour and bicarbonate of soda into a bowl and pour the liquidised mixture over.
Mix on speed 2-3 moving beaters through mixture just long enough to combine thoroughly.
Bake in a greased 7" tin for 40 minutes at gas mark 5 or 190 degrees C.

3-LAYER BLUEBERRY & WHITE CHOCOLATE CAKE WITH LEMON & LIME

For the cake:
400g butter.
400g Fairtrade caster sugar.
200g Fairtrade white chocolate, broken into pieces.
400g self- raising flour.
7 large free-range eggs.
30g locally grown blueberries.
1 lemon, zest and juice.
1 lime, zest and juice.

For the icing:
200g butter.
250g Fairtrade icing sugar.
Juice of half a lemon and half a lime.

Method: Cake:
Pre-heat the oven to gas mark 4 or 180 degrees C.
Grease and line 3 x 9-inch (23cm) cake tins.
Put the butter and the chocolate into a heat-proof bowl over a pan of simmering water and allow to slowly melt whilst stirring. When the chocolate and butter have melted, remove and allow to cool for 5-10 minutes.
Beat in the eggs and sugar.
Stir in the lemon and lime juice and zest.
Fold in the flour and some of the blueberries, leaving enough for decoration later.
Pour the mixture evenly into the 3 tins and bake for around 30 mins or until a skewer inserted comes out cleanly.
Cool in the tins for 10 minutes, turn out onto a wire rack.

3-LAYER BLUEBERRY & WHITE CHOCOLATE CAKE
WITH LEMON & LIME

See Front Cover

Method: Icing:
Beat all the ingredients together and leave to cool in the fridge until the cakes have cooled completely.
Sandwich the layers together with the icing and put a thin layer on top.
Decorate with more blueberries, slices of lemon and lime and a drizzle of white chocolate.

APPLE & ALMOND LAYER CAKE

150g sunflower margarine.
2 large free-range eggs, beaten.
225g Fairtrade golden granulated sugar.
1 teaspoon almond essence.
225g self raising flour, sifted.
1 ½ teaspoons baking powder.
350g cooking apples, peeled, cored and sliced.
25g flaked almonds.

Method:
Beat the margarine and sugar together.
Add eggs, flour and baking powder.
Add almond essence a drop at a time whilst stirring.
Beat thoroughly until well combined.

Spread half the mixture into a greased 20cm loose-bottomed cake tin.
Cover with the sliced apples.
Put the remaining cake mixture on top of the apples in blobs.
Sprinkle with flaked almonds.
Bake in oven gas mark 3, 160 degrees C, for about 1 ½ hours, until golden and the edges shrink away from the sides of the tin.
Turn out onto a wire rack to cool.

Can be served warm with whipped cream or custard.

SWISS ROLL

75g self-raising flour.
110g Fairtrade caster sugar.
25g melted butter or margarine.
3 large free-range eggs.
1 tablespoon hot water.
Strawberry jam.

Method:
Mix the eggs and sugar in a basin and whisk till thick.
Fold in sieved flour with a metal spoon.
Fold in water and butter/margarine.
Bake in a large rectangular tin, lined with greased paper, for
7 minutes at Gas mark 7 or 220 degress C.
Turn onto sugared paper.
Cut off crisp edges.
Spread with jam and roll firmly.

STICKY GINGER CAKE

For the cake:
200g butter.
150g Fairtrade dark muscovado sugar.
100g black treacle.
4 balls stem ginger, chopped.
2 large free-range eggs, beaten.
200g self-raising flour.
1 teaspoon bicarbonate of soda.
1 teaspoon ground ginger.
1 teaspoon ground cinnamon.
225ml yoghurt.

For the icing:
Icing sugar, ground ginger and water.

Method:
Grease a tin, preferably ring or bundt.
Heat the butter, treacle and sugar in a saucepan.
Beat in the eggs and chopped ginger.
Add to sifted dry ingredients, stir and add yoghurt.
Pour into tin and bake at gas mark 4, 180 degrees C, for about 50 minutes.
(Less if using a ring tin and check after 40 minutes).
Cool in the tin and then turn out onto a wire rack.

Mix icing sugar, ginger and water to a desired thickness and spread over the top of the cake.

STICKY GINGER CAKE

CHOCOLATE FUDGE CAKE

For the cake:

4 free-range large eggs.
225g Fairtrade caster sugar.
225g butter or margarine.
225g self-raising flour.
20g Fairtrade cocoa powder.
1 pinch of baking powder.
2 tablespoons milk.
125g Fairtrade dark chocolate.

For fudge top:

1kg icing sugar.
450g evaporated milk.
500g Fairtrade dark chocolate.

Decoration:

Easter - mini eggs.
Christmas - walnuts, cherries,
Birthdays - sugar craft, candles.

Method:

Heat oven to 180 C or Gas mark 4.

Lightly butter and line the bases of two 18cm sandwich tins with baking paper.

Add all the ingredients. Melt the chocolate and gently fold into the mixture.

Bake for about 30 minutes until sponge is risen and firm but not hard to the touch.

Cool in tin for a few minutes, then turn out onto a wire rack until cold.

For the fudge topping, mix the icing sugar with the evaporated milk. Melt the dark chocolate either in the microwave or using a steamer. Pour the melted dark chocolate into the mix gradually and continue mixing. The icing will become very stiff. Soften this over warm water or using a microwave to make it more workable.

Sandwich the cooled cakes with the fudge mix and also cover top and sides.

This cake can be decorated according to the season such as with Mini Easter Eggs.

LIZ'S BOILED FRUIT CAKE

450g can crushed pineapple.
110g butter or sunflower margarine.
110g Fairtrade caster sugar (brown, white or mixture
of both).
450g Fairtrade dried mixed fruit.
1 level teaspoon bicarbonate of soda.
2 free-range eggs.
110g plain flour.
110g self-raising flour.
1 pinch of salt.

Method:
Combine pineapple (with the juice), butter, sugar and fruit in a
saucepan and simmer for 15 minutes.
Add bicarbonate of soda, stir and allow to cool (makes a frothy mix)
Stir in the eggs.
Fold in the flour and salt.

Pour into greased cake tin and bake at Gas mark 3 or 170 degrees C,
for approximately 1¾ hours.
(cover tin with tin plate, or similar, for first hour).

CHOCOLATE FRIDGE CAKE

225g margarine.
250g condensed milk.
225g digestive biscuits.
175g Fairtrade dried fruit.
175g Fairtrade desiccated coconut.
20g Fairtrade cocoa powder.
225g Fairtrade dark chocolate.

Method:
Over a low heat or in the microwave, melt the margarine.
Add the condensed milk.
Crush the digestive biscuits, this can be done by placing the biscuits broken up in a bag and pressing them with a rolling pin.
Mix all the dry ingredients really well together and then fold them into the condensed milk and margarine mixture.
Grease a small-sided baking tray.
Press the mixture into the greased baking tin.
Melt the dark chocolate in either a microwave oven or over water.
Cover the cold cake mix with the melted chocolate.
Sprinkle with the coconut.
Put into a fridge until set.
Cut into squares.

For Rocky Road Fridge Cake add in 100g of marshmallows, either small ones or large cut up.

APPLE SCONES

300g self-raising flour.
75g margarine or butter.
75g Fairtrade caster sugar.
2 medium sized apples from local farmers' market.
20ml milk from sustainable source.
A pinch of salt.

Method:
Heat oven to 200 C or Gas mark 6.
Lightly grease the base of a baking tray.
Sieve flour and salt into a large bowl.
Rub in the margarine until the mix is completely even and lump free.
Add sugar and grated apple and enough milk to give a soft dough but which is not too sticky.
Shape into circles and place on the greased baking tray.

Brush the top with milk and sprinkle with sugar.
Bake for about 20-30 minutes until the scones have risen and are golden brown.
Remove from the oven. Cool on the baking tray for 5 minutes.
Turn out onto a wire rack until cold.

GINGERBREAD

225g Fairtrade soft brown sugar.
180g butter.
450g organic wholemeal flour.
1 level tablespoon of ground ginger.
1 level tablespoon of baking powder.
1 pinch of bicarbonate of soda.
1 pinch of salt.
170g black treacle.
170g golden syrup.
250ml milk.
1 large free-range egg.

Method:
Heat oven to 180 C or Gas mark 4.
Grease a 9 inch (23cm) square cake tin, about 2 inches (50mm) deep and line with buttered greaseproof paper.
Mix all the ingredients well in a mixing bowl.
Warm the sugar, butter, black treacle, golden syrup in a pan over low heat until the butter has just melted.
Stir the melted ingredients into the dry mixture, mixing thoroughly.
Add the milk and beaten egg. Mix thoroughly.
Pour the mixture into the prepared tin and bake in the warm oven for 1½ hours until well risen and firm to the touch.
Allow to cool in the tin for 15 minutes, then turn out onto a wire rack.
Gingerbread is best stored in an airtight tin for a few days to allow the flavour to develop.

BISCUITS & COOKIES

TIFFIN

450g crushed digestive biscuits.
2 tablespoons Fairtrade caster sugar.
2 tablespoons golden syrup.
1 tablespoon Fairtrade cocoa.
225g sunflower margarine.
110g Fairtrade sultanas.
175g Fairtrade plain chocolate.

Method:
Melt the sugar, syrup and margarine in a saucepan.
Stir in the cocoa, sultanas and crushed biscuits.
Mix well.
Press firmly into a large tray-bake tin.
Allow to cool.
Cover with melted chocolate.

When cold, cut into about 24 pieces.

NUT, FRUIT & LEMON BISCUITS

225g organic porridge oats.
170g organic wholemeal flour.
280g butter or margarine.
120g of Fairtrade soft brown sugar.
Half a teaspoon of baking powder.
120g of chopped nuts.
170g of Fairtrade mixed dried fruit.
5g of local honey.
Grated zest and juice of two lemons.

Method:
Heat oven to 180 C or Gas mark 4.
Lightly grease a large baking tray.
Mix all dry ingredients in a large bowl.
In a saucepan melt butter and honey then add to the dry ingredients.
Grate the zest of the lemon and squeeze the juice, adding to the dry mix.
Mix thoroughly. Make small circles onto the greased baking tray, ensuring they do not touch.
Bake for about 25- 30 minutes until golden brown and firm but not hard to the touch.
Cool in the baking tin for 5 minutes, then turn out onto a wire rack until cold.
Store in an airtight container. The biscuits will keep for several days.
Uncooked dough can be stored in the fridge for up to a week or for longer in a freezer.

OAT BISCUITS

175g of Fairtrade self-raising flour.
200g of Fairtrade or organic porridge oats.
125g of Fairtrade soft brown sugar.
120g of butter.
A pinch of baking powder.
1 pinch of salt.
1 teaspoon of mixed spices.   .

Method:
Heat oven to 180 C or Gas mark 4.
Lightly grease a large baking tray.
Soften the butter.
Cream butter and sugar together in a bowl.
Stir in the flour, oats, spices and mix really well.
Cut up the dried cranberries or apricots and add to the mix, stirring thoroughly.
Make into small circles onto the greased baking tray, ensuring they do not touch.
Bake for about 20 minutes until golden brown and firm but not hard to the touch.
Cool in the baking tin for 5 minutes, then turn out onto a wire rack until cold.
Store in an airtight container, keeping for several days.
Fruit version: Some 250g of Fairtrade dried fruit (raisins, apricots and cranberries) could be added.
Savoury biscuits: Could be made with 50g only of sugar and include curry powder instead of mixed spices.

CHOCOLATE CHIP COOKIES

250g self-raising flour.
150g margarine or butter.
100g caster sugar.
50g chocolate chips.
1 free-range egg.

Method:
Heat oven to 180 C or Gas mark 4.
Lightly grease a baking tray.
Put flour in a bowl and rub in the
butter or margarine until it looks like breadcrumbs.
Stir in the sugar and the chocolate chips.
Whisk the egg and add it to the mix gradually
until it binds together.
Form into balls and place on the greased tray.
Bake for 12 to 15 minutes until golden.
Remove from oven and cool.
Cool in the baking tin for 5 minutes. Turn out onto a wire
rack until cold.
Store in an airtight container, keeping several days.

DATE BARS

Ingredients:
For the date and spice mixture:

230g chopped stoned dates.
Zest and juice of a lemon.
Half a teaspoon of ground cinnamon.
Half a teaspoon of mixed spice.

For the oat dough mixture:

60g golden syrup.
180g of margarine.
70g of organic rolled oats.
100g of plain flour.
100g of Fairtrade soft brown sugar.

Method:
Heat oven to 180 C or Gas mark 4.
Lightly grease an 8 inch (20cm) baking tin.
Microwave dates, lemon juice, cinnamon and mixed spice in a
bowl for 1 minute.
Melt margarine and syrup and then mix in the oats, flour and sugar.
Put half of the oat dough mixture into the cake tin.
Spread the date and spice mix evenly over the oat dough.
Place the remaining oat dough mixture evenly over the date and
spice mixture.
Place in the oven already heated to required temperature. Bake for
15 to 20 minutes until golden brown and firm but not hard
to the touch.
Remove from oven and cool in the baking tin for 5 minutes.
Turn out onto a wire rack. When cold cut into bars.
Store in an airtight container to keep for several days.
Uncooked cookie mixture can be stored in the fridge for up to a
week before cooking.

COCONUT SHORTBREAD

225g soft margarine or softened butter.
110g Fairtrade caster sugar.
70g Fairtrade desiccated coconut.
220g organic porridge oats.
220g plain flour.
1 pinch of salt.
1 pinch of baking powder.
2 tablespoons soft brown sugar.

Method:
Heat oven to 150 C or Gas mark 2.
Lightly grease a 9 inch baking tin or similar area tray.
Cream margarine/ butter and sugar.
Sift the flour.
Add dried ingredients, mixing to a uniform consistency.
Spread evenly in the baking tray.
Aim for biscuits about 250 mm thick.
Bake for 1 hour at the required temperature until golden brown and firm but not hard to the touch.
Remove from oven and cut whilst still hot. Dust with brown sugar.
Cool in the tin then turn out onto a wire rack until cold.
Store in an airtight container. The shortbread will keep for several days.

FRUIT & OAT SHORTBREAD

225g margarine or softened butter.   .
110g Fairtrade caster sugar.
110g plain flour.
60g Fairtrade desiccated coconut.
225g organic porridge oats.
225g Fairtrade mixed dried fruit, apricots or cranberries, finely chopped.
1 pinch of salt.
1 pinch of baking powder.

Method:
Heat oven to 150 C or Gas mark 2.
Lightly grease an 9inch baking tin or similar area tray.
Cream margarine/ butter and sugar.
Add all of the other dried ingredients including the dried fruit.
Spread evenly in the baking tray.
Bake for 1 hour at the required temperature until golden brown and firm but not hard to the touch.
Remove from oven and cut whilst still hot. Sprinkle with granulated or brown sugar.
Cool in the tin then turn out onto a wire rack until cold.
Store in an airtight container. The shortbread will keep for several days.
Uncooked cookie mixture can be stored in the fridge for up to a week before cooking.

THE SPIRE APPEAL

The 150 foot Free Church Spire, a prominent landmark in St Ives market place, is undergoing renovation work with the help of money from many people and organisations in the town and surrounding villages. The spire urgently needs stone replacement, repointing and weed removal.

The St Ives Free Church traces its history back to the time of Oliver Cromwell. The current premises were substantially modernised in 1980 to provide a church building that not only services its worshipping community but also serves the town in many ways.

The church supports a well-stocked Fairtrade shop and Tookeys community coffee shop. The building is used by over 25 local organisations for their regular meetings. These include the Volunteer Bureau, RSPB, Civic Society, U3A and many others. It provides an excellent venue for concerts and exhibitions.

Thank you very much for your continued and ongoing support to save our spire.

ACKNOWLEDGEMENTS

The Save Our Spire Appeal Team would like to thank everyone who provided recipes and for the entries for the cake competition at the garden party in July 2017.

Save Our Spire!

Printed in Great Britain
by Amazon